The SELF-ASSESSMENT and PROGRAM REVIEW

SAPRpbis™

for POSITIVE BEHAVIOR INTERVENTIONS and SUPPORTS

Bridget Walker, Ph.D.
and
Douglas Cheney, Ph.D.

PAUL H. BROOKES PUBLISHING CO.®
www.brookespublishing.com

Baltimore • London • Sydney

SAPRpbis™ | Individual Form

School: ______________________ Date: ______________________

Name: ______________________ Position: ______________________

Team meeting date: ______________________

OVERVIEW

The first step of implementing schoolwide positive behavior interventions and supports (PBIS) involves a school self-assessment. Your leadership team will use this self-assessment tool to identify your school's strengths and needs related to evidence-based practices essential to the effective implementation of PBIS. Following each practice is a list of indicators that characterize this practice. Team members will use their ratings to assess the functioning level of the school. Many of the practices in this tool are relevant to every student in the school, whereas others are specifically focused on helping students who may be struggling with emotional or behavioral problems. For those practices that are focused on supporting students who may be struggling, throughout this assessment the term *emotional or behavioral problems (E/BPs)* is used to include all students with challenging behavior, not just those receiving special education services.

INDIVIDUAL SELF-ASSESSMENT DIRECTIONS

You have been asked to complete this form because you are a member of the schoolwide leadership team. Please complete this survey prior to the scheduled team meeting. Look over each item and rate it using the rating scale below; determine the rating based on your specific knowledge and experience in the school. Circle *1* if you are not sure whether your school implements a particular practice as stated; then, share your responses and any questions at the team meeting.

Once you have rated all of the indicators, add the ratings for each practice and place the total in the spaces provided. Please be sure to rate all items. Use the scale that follows to determine your final ratings. Please consider the questions listed in each box to help you finalize your decisions. Circle any indicators that you would particularly like to discuss, and write down any comments or questions that you would like to share with the team. If you have any questions about this process, please talk with the designated facilitator for this process or with your school administrator.

Remember: Please do not discuss or compare ratings with other members of your team until the team meeting.

THE SELF-ASSESSMENT SCALE

5 = This indicator of the evidence-based practice is *fully in place.* Data and documentation indicate that it is functioning well and implemented with a high degree of consistency. The practice requires only maintenance of effort at this time.

4 = This indicator of the evidence-based practice is *mostly in place.* Data and documentation indicate that it is consistently implemented in school practice. However, there may be some issues with the consistency of implementation that suggest it requires additional work to be fully in place.

3 = This indicator of the evidence-based practice is *moderately in place.* Data and documentation indicate that it may only be implemented with consistency about half the time. It is clearly in need of additional work to be fully in place.

2 = This indicator of the evidence-based practice is only *partially in place.* Data and documentation indicate that it is inconsistently implemented and needs much more work to be fully in place.

1 = This indicator of the evidence-based practice is *not yet in place.* Data and documentation indicate that it is rarely implemented with any consistency and will require extensive work before it can be fully in place.

1	Administrative policies and procedures support the education of all students, including those with or at risk of developing E/BPs.		
1.1	**The school or district has a written statement that values the education of all students, including those with E/BPs.** Does your school have a mission statement or overall philosophy that is shared with staff, students, and families through written documents such as the school handbook? If so, does it clearly state a commitment to the success of all learners, including those with learning and/or behavioral problems?	*Notes*	1 2 3 4 5
1.2	**Policies and programs in the school handbook focus on the *prevention* of academic and behavior problems.** Does the school handbook describe strategies, practices, or programs designed to support students before they demonstrate significant academic or behavior problems? Does it explain to students and parents how they can gain access to these practices or programs? Does it explain how these programs can be helpful to students?	*Notes*	1 2 3 4 5
1.3	**Sufficient resources are allocated to implement these policies and programs.** Are enough staff, time, volunteers, and materials available to ensure that these programs and supports are delivered consistently and efficiently?	*Notes*	1 2 3 4 5
1.4	**The school has a leadership team that meets regularly to review schoolwide discipline issues.** Has a team of faculty and staff been created that meets monthly to review data, concerns, and issues related to schoolwide discipline?	*Notes*	1 2 3 4 5
1.5	**The team includes a school administrator, representative staff, educators, and families/community members.** Does the team include the school principal or vice principal and individuals that represent the range of faculty, staff, and community members (including paraprofessionals, general and special educators, counselors, psychologists, and family members)?	*Notes*	1 2 3 4 5
1.6	**The school's leadership team develops annual goals and objectives to improve schoolwide PBIS.** Does this team establish a written plan that outlines priorities at least once a year? Are these plans shared with the full school staff?	*Notes*	1 2 3 4 5
1.7	**The school's leadership team annually evaluates progress on goals and objectives.** Does this team collect data that help it determine whether the plan has been successful? Does the team then adjust the plan as needed?	*Notes*	1 2 3 4 5

Comments or questions for the team:

Total your score for this practice: ________

2	School policies and programs emphasize prevention and the early identification of students with or at risk of developing E/BPs.		
2.1	**A systematic schoolwide screening program is used annually to identify students with or at risk of developing E/BPs.** Does your school have a screening tool, such as the Systematic Screening for Behavior Disorders or the Behavior and Emotional Screening Scale? Is it used in the first 2 months of school to identify students in need of Tier 2 intervention? Are office discipline referrals (ODRs) used to identify students who need extra support?	*Notes*	1 2 3 4 5
2.2	**A teacher assistance or prereferral intervention team is in place and is available in a timely manner to address problem behavior of students.** Does the team meet twice monthly to review student progress and nominate students for additional supports? Does the team have efficient and effective interventions for use with students?	*Notes*	1 2 3 4 5
2.3	**Teams develop a method for ensuring that interventions are implemented with fidelity for all students identified as having E/BPs.** Do the reviews lead to implementation of interventions? Do staff monitor and evaluate the interventions? Do team members visit classrooms to note implementation?	*Notes*	1 2 3 4 5
2.4	**An interpersonal problem-solving approach is taught and used by the entire staff with all students in the building.** Do all school staff know how to discuss interpersonal problems with students? Do they use a multistep approach that identifies the problem, reviews the social expectations of the school, discusses positive solutions, and has students commit to using positive social skills/expectations? Do the faculty and staff review the effectiveness of the approach monthly by reviewing data, concerns, and issues related to the problem-solving approach?	*Notes*	1 2 3 4 5
2.5	**The school counseling program is integrated with PBIS and is available to all students.** Does your school have a school counselor? Is the counselor a member of your PBIS leadership team? Does the counselor help students learn and use the school's social expectations? Can students visit the school counselor for social-interpersonal problem-solving sessions?	*Notes*	1 2 3 4 5
2.6	**Families of students with E/BPs are engaged in school programs.** Does your school have a family involvement program or goal? Do families assist students or teachers in classrooms? Is there an active family leadership group? Do families that are involved with the school contact those that may be hesitant to come to school? Do parents identify professional development activities to help them with their children's education?	*Notes*	1 2 3 4 5

Comments or questions for the team:

Total your score for this practice: ________

3	Staff development activities focus on methods to educate all students, including those with or at risk of developing E/BPs.		
3.1	**Ongoing staff development is provided to address the school's programs for social-emotional development of *all* students.** Do some of the faculty and staff meetings and scheduled in-service days address topics related to social-emotional development of all students? If so, how often? How useful is the content presented? Does the staff development relate directly to schoolwide PBIS?	*Notes*	1 2 3 4 5
3.2	**In-service training focuses on evidence-based practices regarding behavior management strategies for students with or at risk of developing E/BPs.** Does the training content include research-based strategies that are directly useful in the school and classroom? Do the strategies seem consistent with schoolwide PBIS? Do the strategies improve students' social behavior and reduce behavior problems?	*Notes*	1 2 3 4 5
3.3	**In-service training focuses on effective accommodations and instructional modifications for students with or at risk of developing E/BPs.** Does the training include information on strategies to adjust academic and social activities to support success for students with E/BPs? Do the strategies support differentiating within the setting or activity so that all students can be successful?	*Notes*	1 2 3 4 5
3.4	**In-service training focuses on risk and protective factors for the social development of all students.** Does the training include information about how schools can make a difference and support success for students who are at risk?	*Notes*	1 2 3 4 5
3.5	**In-service training focuses on understanding common behavioral disorders of students (e.g., autism, attention deficit disorder, bipolar disorder) and effective supports.** Does the training include helpful information for understanding the definition, issues, and challenges experienced by students with specific disorders and provide effective supports and strategies?	*Notes*	1 2 3 4 5
3.6	**A method is used to evaluate in-service effectiveness.** After the training, are faculty and staff asked to provide feedback on its effectiveness and applicability to your situation?	*Notes*	1 2 3 4 5

Comments or questions for the team:

Total your score for this practice: ________

4	Clear and consistent behavioral expectations are established for students across all school settings.		
4.1	**Staff have adopted or developed a program to teach pro-social skills in classroom and nonclassroom settings.** Does your school have a set of social expectations that are useful throughout the school? Do teachers take time to instruct students in the expectations and behaviors for these settings across the school? Does everyone know how to demonstrate, role-play, and teach social skills?	*Notes*	1 2 3 4 5
4.2	**This program is described in the school handbook.** Does the school handbook describe strategies, practices, or programs to teach social expectations? Does it explain to students and parents how these practices or programs are implemented in classrooms?	*Notes*	1 2 3 4 5
4.3	**Behavioral expectations are written and posted in class-room and nonclassroom settings.** Are there posters throughout your school with your schoolwide social or behavioral expectations? Are they positive and engaging to students? Are students involved in developing or maintaining the posters?	*Notes*	1 2 3 4 5
4.4	**Behavioral expectations are taught, monitored, and re-inforced systematically in classroom and nonclassroom settings.** Is there a plan to teach social and behavioral expectations during the first day, week, and month of school, across all school set-tings? Are additional booster sessions taught throughout the year?	*Notes*	1 2 3 4 5
4.5	**Teachers and staff use effective approaches to discourage problem behavior.** Do teachers give warnings, prompts, and redirections when they see misbehavior? Do the staff practice and use verbal problem-solving approaches for minor problems? Do teachers reinforce peers demonstrating responsible behavior when they see misbe-havior in the classroom?	*Notes*	1 2 3 4 5
4.6	**The school leadership team monitors and evaluates the impact of the schoolwide program.** Does the team review its data frequently and give feedback to the staff? Are there celebrations when the staff meet goals?	*Notes*	1 2 3 4 5
4.7	**The behavioral expectations and schoolwide program are regularly communicated to families.** Do families receive newsletters, e-mails, or postings on web sites to learn about progress in schoolwide social programs? Is progress discussed at schoolwide family meetings such as parent nights at school?	*Notes*	1 2 3 4 5

Comments or questions for the team:

Total your score for this practice: ___________

5	School procedures for responding to discipline referrals and emergency situations are implemented consistently and effectively.		
5.1	**The discipline process includes criteria for office referrals, addressing the behavior of concern, and returning the student to the classroom.** Does a clear, consistently implemented process exist? Is it written down? Are all students, faculty, staff, and families aware of the process? Is it followed consistently?	*Notes*	1 2 3 4 5
5.2	**Discipline and suspension policies are clearly stated in the handbook and effectively communicated to parents, students, and staff.** Does a written statement of the policies exist? Are the consequences for certain behaviors clearly defined? Is the statement available in all the languages of the student community? Does everyone understand and follow the written process?	*Notes*	1 2 3 4 5
5.3	**Discipline procedures meet state and federal regulatory requirements (e.g., use functional behavioral assessments [FBAs] and behavior intervention plans [BIPs] when appropriate, employ documentation and parent contact as required).** Are all of the policies and procedures related to discipline aligned with regulations? Do students who qualify for special education due to behavioral problems have an effective FBA and BIP in place? Does everyone involved in discipline understand federal and state laws related to reporting and implementing discipline?	*Notes*	1 2 3 4 5
5.4	**Staff with specialized training are available to help resolve students' social-emotional conflicts.** Have some or all of your staff members been formally trained to respond to and help students who are having difficulties, and are they available to help such students calm down and/or talk about their problems? Does the method used align with PBIS?	*Notes*	1 2 3 4 5
5.5	**A designated area is available in the office, hallway, or a classroom to resolve students' social-emotional problems (e.g., a problem-solving area, think time area, cool-off spot, buddy room).** *Note:* This is *not* a reference to a time-out room. Are there supervised places where students can be sent when a problem is starting, where they can refocus, calm down, and make a plan to get back on track? Is this system used consistently and effectively?	*Notes*	1 2 3 4 5
5.6	**A team of teachers and staff is trained to use a crisis prevention and intervention program for emergency situations.** Have some staff members been specifically trained in responding to crisis situations and helping students de-escalate in a way that protects student and staff safety if needed? Is the approach used in alignment with PBIS?	*Notes*	1 2 3 4 5

Comments or questions for the team:

Total your score for this practice: ________

6	Systematic supports are developed to address the academic and social needs of students with E/BPs.		
6.1	**General educators receive support in their classrooms from certified specialists experienced with students having E/BPs (e.g., school psychologist, school counselor, behavior specialist, special educator).** Does your school attempt to improve the social and academic environment by having specialists work collaboratively and purposefully in general education classrooms? Are time and resources allocated so that prescribed programs can be effectively implemented in classrooms?	*Notes*	1 2 3 4 5
6.2	**Tier 2 behavior interventions or support plans are developed for students with E/BPs.** Does the student support team (SST) have time to meet and collaboratively develop behavior plans for students? Does the team help with professional development so that the plan can be coordinated across staff and implemented with fidelity?	*Notes*	1 2 3 4 5
6.3	**Academic supports help students with E/BPs receive passing grades in their classes.** Are either teacher-mediated or peer-mediated academic supports available, such as small-group instruction, classwide peer tutoring, or cross-age tutoring? Do teachers adapt materials in terms of length and time allowable for completion? Are the academic supports monitored for effectiveness? Do struggling students seem to benefit from the supports provided?	*Notes*	1 2 3 4 5
6.4	**Specialized services such as a focused prosocial skills training help students with E/BPs succeed socially and behaviorally.** Is there a Tier 2 intervention system that uses a check-in and check-out process, a daily progress report card, social skills instruction, problem solving, or another approach? Are these implemented and coordinated across the school's specialists and teachers?	*Notes*	1 2 3 4 5
6.5	**Instructional approaches (e.g., Behavior Education Program; Check, Connect, and Expect; check-in and check-out process) are used to address individual students' cognitive, behavioral, and emotional needs.** Do you have a special educator or a coach for students who understands and assists in social or academic modifications and accommodations? Does he or she help you understand how to break concepts into understandable units and how to make activities more meaningful to students who are unengaged in instruction? Does the social coach see students daily for checking in, monitoring daily progress, and checking out at day's end?	*Notes*	1 2 3 4 5

6	Systematic supports are developed to address the academic and social needs of students with E/BPs. *(continued)*		
6.6	**Social supports facilitate positive interpersonal relationships for students with E/BPs (e.g., circle of friends, buddy system, peer mentors).** Are peer-to-peer networks organized such that students help one another? Does instruction help enhance friendships and social interactions? Do staff teach the value of friendship and identify peers who will be helpful and empathic with students who have social difficulties? Are mentor systems in place to help struggling students?	*Notes*	1 2 3 4 5

Comments or questions for the team:

Total your score for this practice: ________

7	FBAs are completed for students with significant behavior problems to develop intensive interventions.		
7.1	**The team uses FBA procedures for developing students' BIPs.** Does an FBA team include staff with behavioral expertise for the FBA process? Does the team meet regularly to develop plans for students with behavior problems? Does the team identify the function of the student's behavior and then develop a proactive behavior plan that uses function-based interventions to teach students new skills to be successful?	*Notes*	1 2 3 4 5
7.2	**Each behavior plan addresses setting events, antecedents, prosocial skills, positive reinforcement, and the function of the behavior.** Does the team understand the components of a student's behavior pattern and understand ways to help the student learn more appropriate behaviors for meeting the behavioral function? Do the BIPs include strategies for teaching the student prosocial skills and detail how adults will reinforce these new skills?	*Notes*	1 2 3 4 5
7.3	**BIPs are developed collaboratively with family members and are sensitive to cultural and linguistic differences.** Are family members and caregivers included in the development of the plans? Are team members aware of the cultural, gender, and linguistic issues related to discipline and student behavior? Are positive behavior plans developed that feel supportive to the student and family members as well as school staff?	*Notes*	1 2 3 4 5
7.4	**BIPs include systematic data collection to assess student progress.** Do all behavior plans include clear strategies for tracking and monitoring the student's problem behaviors and prosocial skills to determine whether the plan is effective? Are changes made to the plan when necessary based on collected data?	*Notes*	1 2 3 4 5
7.5	**A case manager coordinates and monitors the BIP for each student.** Are the plans followed by a trained staff member who helps to ensure that the plan is followed consistently and helps to answer questions and solve problems as they occur?	*Notes*	1 2 3 4 5

Comments or questions for the team:

Total your score for this practice: ________

8	Data are routinely collected and systematically analyzed by the leadership team for program-evaluation and decision-making purposes.		
8.1	**Staff collect and analyze patterns in ODRs using an electronic database.** Does your school have an established referral process for disciplinary actions? Does it distinguish between minor problems that are classroom managed and major problems that are handled by an administrator? Are data collected on ODRs and analyzed by the leadership team or SST?	*Notes*	1 2 3 4 5
8.2	**Reports from the database are reviewed monthly to analyze patterns.** Does the leadership or SST give reports to staff regarding ODRs and other behavioral issues or successes at least monthly? Are the reports used to improve the school's PBIS approach?	*Notes*	1 2 3 4 5
8.3	**Staff collect and analyze information on students' social and academic behavior in classrooms and nonclassroom settings.** Are grades and other academic indicators, ODRs, or daily progress report (DPR) data used by classroom teachers and staff to improve the overall functioning of students in classroom and nonclassroom settings? Do the teachers and staff think these are meaningful data for improving academic and social functioning of students?	*Notes*	1 2 3 4 5
8.4	**Data are analyzed to evaluate the relationship between ethnicity and disciplinary actions (e.g., referrals, suspensions, expulsions).** Does the SST disaggregate data to look at issues of disproportionality based on race or ethnicity? Are any of the findings used to change practice regarding multicultural competence? Does the SST or administrator conduct professional development to address multicultural competence?	*Notes*	1 2 3 4 5
8.5	**ODR data are analyzed in the screening process to identify students with or at risk of developing E/BPs.** Does the SST use ODRs or other screening tools to identify those students in need of Tier 2 intervention? Are the data looked at monthly to make this determination?	*Notes*	1 2 3 4 5
8.6	**ODR data are considered when developing intervention plans for students.** Are the types of ODRs (e.g., disruptive, defiant, aggressive) reviewed to determine behavioral function? Are interventions matched with the type of behavioral difficulty to enhance efficiency and effectiveness?	*Notes*	1 2 3 4 5

Comments or questions for the team:

Total your score for this practice: ________

9	Families are seen as partners in the development of their child's program.		
9.1	**Family members are part of each child's team and are encouraged to participate in meetings and school activities.** When students begin to have trouble at school, are parents and/or caregivers immediately notified and included in the problem-solving process? Are family members invited to be team members? Are family members encouraged to join other relevant school teams? Are family members welcome in classrooms during the instructional day?	*Notes*	1 2 3 4 5
9.2	**Parents of children with significant behavioral concerns have access to a family support group when needed.** Are there supports available for families whose students are struggling significantly in school (e.g., parent network, community group)? Do school staff help connect families to these supports?	*Notes*	1 2 3 4 5
9.3	**Families are supported in gaining access to additional community resources.** When families need information on additional supports (e.g., health services, food or clothing bank, child care, recreational options), do school staff provide information and help families connect with these supports?	*Notes*	1 2 3 4 5
9.4	**Family education programs and resources are available at the school.** Does the school include references, resources, and supports to help families and students experience success (e.g., parent library, parent network, effective parenting strategies)? Do these programs occur at your school or in the community? Do school staff assist families in connecting with and participating in the programs?	*Notes*	1 2 3 4 5
9.5	**A family's cultural and community perspective is valued and integrated into communication and student supports.** Does the school provide information, materials, resources, and events that are meaningful and accessible to the various cultural groups within the school community? Are these events and resources translated so that they are accessible to families who speak other languages? Do school events, meetings, and activities reflect and respect the cultural traditions that make up the school community?	*Notes*	1 2 3 4 5

Comments or questions for the team:

Total your score for this practice: __________

10	Comprehensive plans are developed for students and families in need of intensive support.		
10.1	**Students with severe behavior problems have timely access to medical, mental health, and other community social services.** Does your school have connections with local service providers? Are these connections formal or informal agreements? Do the representatives of these agencies come to meetings at your school? Is your school nurse or school psychologist able to connect and coordinate services with these other private or public providers?	*Notes*	1 2 3 4 5
10.2	**A student's use of prescription medication is known by staff and is monitored frequently by school and family members.** Does your school nurse, psychologist, or administrator have an understanding and documentation of medications used by students? Does someone know about the effects and side effects of the medications? Is there some form of monitoring of prescribed medications in the school?	*Notes*	1 2 3 4 5
10.3	**Students with individualized education programs (IEPs) have goals and objectives for their social and emotional needs.** Are social-emotional assessments linked to the IEP? Are the goals for social-emotional development on the IEP measurable, and do they contain benchmarks for progress monitoring? Do behavior plans use methods to accomplish these goals?	*Notes*	1 2 3 4 5
10.4	**Professionals from other agencies serve on students' IEP teams as needed.** Is there a wraparound process for students who have complex or intensive needs? Do representatives from other agencies attend IEP or other planning meetings? Are these other professionals providing appropriate services to meet students' needs?	*Notes*	1 2 3 4 5
10.5	**The school or district has a formal agreement with community agencies to provide services to meet the needs of students and their families.** Have district or school administrators formalized any service agreements with medical, mental health, and other community social services for students with severe behavior problems? Are services determined by a multidisciplinary team including family members, a district or school administrator, educators, and community agency members?	*Notes*	1 2 3 4 5
10.6	**Interagency teams develop, implement, and evaluate treatment plans that are family centered, based on strengths and needs, and sensitive to cultural and linguistic differences.** When there is an interagency team, does it use the wraparound process to develop a comprehensive treatment plan for the student? Is it person and family centered and culturally competent for the student and family?	*Notes*	1 2 3 4 5

10	Comprehensive plans are developed for students and families in need of intensive support. *(continued)*		
10.7	**A family support liaison regularly contacts parents of students in need of intensive support.** Does anyone in the school or district serve as a liaison to families and/or community agencies? Can members of the faculty assume responsibility for working with individual families?	*Notes*	1 2 3 4 5
10.8	**A case manager coordinates all communication between the interagency team members.** Is there a case manager for students who have multiple agency representation? Does the case manager coordinate, communicate, and evaluate multiagency care?	*Notes*	1 2 3 4 5

Comments or questions for the team:

Total your score for this practice: ________

SAPRpbis™ | Team Meeting Form

School: ____________________ District: ____________________

Team meeting date: ____________________ Meeting facilitator: ____________________

Leadership team members: ____________________

OVERVIEW

The first step of schoolwide program improvement involves a school self-assessment. This self-assessment tool was developed to assess evidence-based practices regarding schoolwide discipline, data collection, family and community involvement, and individualized student supports related to the effective implementation of positive behavior support. Your team will use this self-assessment tool to identify your school's strengths and needs related to these practices. This self-assessment contains a list of evidence-based practices for students with challenging behavior. Following each practice is a list of elements that characterize this practice. Team members will use their rating to assess the functioning level of the school. Many of the practices in this tool are relevant to every student in the school, whereas others are specifically focused on helping students who may be struggling with emotional or behavioral problems. For those practices that are focused on supporting students who may be struggling, throughout this assessment the term *emotional or behavioral problems* (E/BPs) is used to include all students with challenging behavior, not just those receiving special education services. It is suggested that a PBIS leadership team complete this process at least annually. Once the team has completed the self-assessment process, it uses the data to develop an action plan. *The SAPR-PBIS™ Manual* includes detailed instructions, samples, and other supports for this process.

TEAM ASSESSMENT DIRECTIONS

Step One: Plan for the Self-Assessment Team Meeting

Set a date for the schoolwide PBIS leadership team to meet and complete the Individual Form. The team will need approximately 60–90 minutes to complete the process.

Step Two: Prepare for the Self-Assessment Team Meeting

Prior to the team meeting, each team member should be given the Individual Form to complete and bring with him or her to the team meeting. Specific directions for completing the Individual Form are included on that form, and details are provided in *The SAPR-PBIS™ Manual.* It is recommended that one member of the team be identified to facilitate the team meeting. The facilitator should serve as the team's recorder and will record the final ratings on this form, along with relevant comments and questions for each indicator. The facilitator should also collect current data on such things as office discipline referrals (ODRs), referrals to student support teams, and other practices referenced in the self-assessment discussion for the team's reference throughout the meeting. Documentation such as program descriptions and school policy manuals should also be referenced as part of the final rating process.

Step Three: Conduct the Self-Assessment Team Meeting

As a school leadership team, you will discuss the results of each member's completed Individual Form to develop a consensus about how your school is functioning on the 10 evidence-based practices listed. For each practice, the facilitator asks each team member to share his or her total score from the Individual Form and records that along the scoring bar located under each item. As a team, discuss to what degree each practice is being utilized in your school, based on the scores being reported and the current data related to each practice.

If there is a significant discrepancy between various team members' individual scores, we suggest that the team then discuss the ratings given to each of the indicators listed under the practice to clarify the different perspectives and come to a consensus. See Chapter 4 in the manual for detailed instructions and suggestions for how your team can come to consensus on the rating for a practice.

Step Four: Identify Priorities for Improvement

As a team, review the results of the team assessment to identify up to three evidence-based practices to focus on improving during the school year as part of your schoolwide PBIS program. Use the indicators listed with each evidence-based practice to help you develop specific, measurable objectives for improvement. In the Action Plan on the final page of this form, record these objectives, briefly summarize the activities related to addressing each objective, and outline a plan for measuring progress. Throughout the year, the leadership team should revisit these objectives to determine the progress being made toward achieving them. See the manual for suggestions for developing effective goals and objectives as well as resources for strengthening each practice.

Step Five: Share the Action Plan with School Faculty

Copies of the Action Plan should be given to each PBIS leadership team member for reference. We also suggest that you share these objectives and activities with the entire faculty.

TEAM ASSESSMENT SCALE

(A detailed description for rating each practice is provided in *The SAPR-PBIS™ Manual* in Chapter 5.)

5 = This indicator of the evidence-based practice is *fully in place.* Data and documentation indicate that it is functioning well and implemented with a high degree of consistency. The practice requires only maintenance of effort at this time.

4 = This indicator of the evidence-based practice is *mostly in place.* Data and documentation indicate that most of it is consistently implemented in school practice. However, there may be some issues with the consistency of implementation that suggest it requires additional work to be fully in place.

3 = This indicator of the evidence-based practice is *moderately in place.* Data and documentation indicate that it may only be implemented with consistency about half the time. It is clearly in need of additional work to be fully in place.

2 = This indicator of the evidence-based practice is only *partially in place.* Data and documentation indicate that it is inconsistently implemented and needs much more work to be fully in place.

1 = This indicator of the evidence-based practice is *not yet in place.* Data and documentation indicate that it is rarely implemented with any consistency and will require extensive work before it can be fully in place.

EXAMPLE OF TEAM SCORING PROCESS

5	**School procedures for responding to discipline referrals and emergency situations are implemented consistently and effectively.**
5.1	The discipline process includes criteria for office referrals, addressing the behavior of concern, and returning the student to the classroom.
5.2	Discipline and suspension policies are clearly stated in the handbook and effectively communicated to parents, students, and staff.
5.3	Discipline procedures meet state and federal regulatory requirements (e.g., use functional behavioral assessments [FBAs] and behavior intervention plans [BIPs] when appropriate, employ documentation and parent contact as required).
5.4	Staff with specialized training are available to help resolve students' social-emotional conflicts.
5.5	A designated area is available in the office, hallway, or a classroom to resolve students' social-emotional problems (e.g., a problem-solving area, think time area, cool-off spot, buddy room). *Note:* This is *not* a reference to a time-out room.
5.6	A team of teachers and staff is trained to use a crisis prevention and intervention program for emergency situations.

Outliers

Tally marks represent scores from team members. Circle the range with the most scores. You may circle the overlap between two boxes if applicable.

✓ ✓	✓	✓✓✓✓	✓	
6–10 1 = Not yet in place	**11–15** 2 = Partially in place	**16–20** 3 = Moderately in place	**21–26** 4 = Mostly in place	**27–30** 5 = Fully in place

Note: The top numbers in bold represent the range of total scores from the Individual Form (e.g., 6 questions with 1–5 possible points equals a range of 6–30). The bottom numbers correspond with the rating scale, allowing the team to see where its total scores fall along that scale.

Place a tally mark above the box that includes the total score reported for the practice. If there is a significant discrepancy between ratings, or a low overall score, discuss the individual scores for each of the indicators in order to come to a consensus on the team rating and to identify priorities for improvement. In addition, record any specific questions, ideas, or comments that emerge from the discussion that the team would like to be able to reference in the future. See *The SAPR-PBIS™ Manual* for more suggestions about facilitating this discussion.

1	**Administrative policies and procedures support the education of all students, including those with or at risk of developing E/BPs.**
1.1	The school or district has a written statement that values the education of all students, including those with E/BPs.
1.2	Policies and programs in the school handbook focus on the *prevention* of academic and behavior problems.
1.3	Sufficient resources are allocated to implement these policies and programs.
1.4	The school has a leadership team that meets regularly to review schoolwide discipline issues.
1.5	The team includes a school administrator, representative staff, educators, and families/community members.
1.6	The school's leadership team develops annual goals and objectives to improve schoolwide PBIS.
1.7	The school's leadership team annually evaluates progress on goals and objectives.

Place a tally mark to reflect each of the scores of individual team members, and circle the box that reflects the scores from most team members. If there is a significant discrepancy or a very low score, discuss the individual scores of the indicators to help to develop consensus.

7–12 1 = Not yet in place	**13–18** 2 = Partially in place	**19–24** 3 = Moderately in place	**25–30** 4 = Mostly in place	**31–35** 5 = Fully in place

Notes and comments from the team:

2	**School policies and programs emphasize prevention and the early identification of students with or at risk of developing E/BPs.**
2.1	A systematic schoolwide screening program is used annually to identify students with or at risk of developing E/BPs.
2.2	A teacher assistance or prereferral intervention team is in place and is available in a timely manner to address problem behavior of students.
2.3	Teams develop a method for ensuring that interventions are implemented with fidelity for all students identified as having E/BPs.
2.4	An interpersonal problem-solving approach is taught and used by the entire staff with all students in the building.
2.5	The school counseling program is integrated with PBIS and is available to all students.
2.6	Families of students with E/BPs are engaged in school programs.

Place a tally mark to reflect each of the scores of individual team members, and circle the box that reflects the scores from most team members. If there is a significant discrepancy or a very low score, discuss the individual scores of the indicators to help to develop consensus.

6–9 1 = Not yet in place	**10–15** 2 = Partially in place	**16–20** 3 = Moderately in place	**21–26** 4 = Mostly in place	**27–30** 5 = Fully in place

Notes and comments from the team:

3	**Staff development activities focus on methods to educate all students, including those with or at risk of developing E/BPs.**
3.1	Ongoing staff development is provided to address the school's programs for social-emotional development of *all* students.
3.2	In-service training focuses on evidence-based practices regarding behavior management strategies for students with or at risk of developing E/BPs.
3.3	In-service training focuses on effective accommodations and instructional modifications for students with or at risk of developing E/BPs.
3.4	In-service training focuses on risk and protective factors for the social development of all students.
3.5	In-service training focuses on understanding common behavioral disorders of students (e.g., autism, attention deficit disorder, bipolar disorder) and effective supports.
3.6	A method is used to evaluate in-service effectiveness.

Place a tally mark to reflect each of the scores of individual team members, and circle the box that reflects the scores from most team members. If there is a significant discrepancy or a very low score, discuss the individual scores of the indicators to help to develop consensus.

6–9 1 = Not yet in place	**10–15** 2 = Partially in place	**16–20** 3 = Moderately in place	**21–26** 4 = Mostly in place	**27–30** 5 = Fully in place

Notes and comments from the team:

4	**Clear and consistent behavioral expectations are established for students across all school settings.**
4.1	Staff have adopted or developed a program to teach prosocial skills in classroom and nonclass-room settings.
4.2	This program is described in the school handbook.
4.3	Behavioral expectations are written and posted in classroom and nonclassroom settings.
4.4	Behavioral expectations are taught, monitored, and reinforced systematically in classroom and nonclassroom settings.
4.5	Teachers and staff use effective approaches to discourage problem behavior.
4.6	The school leadership team monitors and evaluates the impact of the schoolwide program.
4.7	The behavioral expectations and schoolwide program are regularly communicated to families.

Place a tally mark to reflect each of the scores of individual team members, and circle the box that reflects the scores from most team members. If there is a significant discrepancy or a very low score, discuss the individual scores of the indicators to help to develop consensus.

7–12 1 = Not yet in place	**13–18** 2 = Partially in place	**19–24** 3 = Moderately in place	**25–30** 4 = Mostly in place	**31–35** 5 = Fully in place

Notes and comments from the team:

5	**School procedures for responding to discipline referrals and emergency situations are implemented consistently and effectively.**
5.1	The discipline process includes criteria for office referrals, addressing the behavior of concern, and returning the student to the classroom.
5.2	Discipline and suspension policies are clearly stated in the handbook and effectively communicated to parents, students, and staff.
5.3	Discipline procedures meet state and federal regulatory requirements (e.g., use functional behavioral assessments [FBAs] and behavior intervention plans [BIPs] when appropriate, employ documentation and parent contact as required).
5.4	Staff with specialized training are available to help resolve students' social-emotional conflicts.
5.5	A designated area is available in the office, hallway, or a classroom to resolve students' social-emotional problems (e.g., a problem-solving area, think time area, cool-off spot, buddy room). *Note:* This is *not* a reference to a time-out room.
5.6	A team of teachers and staff is trained to use a crisis prevention and intervention program for emergency situations.

Place a tally mark to reflect each of the scores of individual team members, and circle the box that reflects the scores from most team members. If there is a significant discrepancy or a very low score, discuss the individual scores of the indicators to help to develop consensus.

6–9 1 = Not yet in place	**10–15** 2 = Partially in place	**16–20** 3 = Moderately in place	**21–26** 4 = Mostly in place	**27–30** 5 = Fully in place

Notes and comments from the team:

6	**Systematic supports are developed to address the academic and social needs of students with E/BPs.**
6.1	General educators receive support in their classrooms from certified specialists experienced with students having E/BPs (e.g., school psychologist, school counselor, behavior specialist, special educator).
6.2	Tier 2 behavior interventions or support plans are developed for students with E/BPs.
6.3	Academic supports help students with E/BPs receive passing grades in their classes.
6.4	Specialized services such as a focused prosocial skills training help students with E/BPs succeed socially and behaviorally.
6.5	Instructional approaches (e.g., Behavior Education Program; Check, Connect, and Expect; check-in and check-out process) are used to address individual students' cognitive, behavioral, and emotional needs.
6.6	Social supports facilitate positive interpersonal relationships for students with E/BPs (e.g., circle of friends, buddy system, peer mentors).

Place a tally mark to reflect each of the scores of individual team members, and circle the box that reflects the scores from most team members. If there is a significant discrepancy or a very low score, discuss the individual scores of the indicators to help to develop consensus.

6–9 1 = Not yet in place	**10–15** 2 = Partially in place	**16–20** 3 = Moderately in place	**21–26** 4 = Mostly in place	**27–30** 5 = Fully in place

Notes and comments from the team:

7	**FBAs are completed for students with significant behavior problems to develop intensive interventions.**
7.1	The team uses FBA procedures for developing students' BIPs.
7.2	Each behavior plan addresses setting events, antecedents, prosocial skills, positive reinforcement, and the function of the behavior.
7.3	BIPs are developed collaboratively with family members and are sensitive to cultural and linguistic differences.
7.4	BIPs include systematic data collection to assess student progress.
7.5	A case manager coordinates and monitors the BIP for each student.

Place a tally mark to reflect each of the scores of individual team members, and circle the box that reflects the scores from most team members. If there is a significant discrepancy or a very low score, discuss the individual scores of the indicators to help to develop consensus.

5–8 1 = Not yet in place	**9–12** 2 = Partially in place	**13–17** 3 = Moderately in place	**18–21** 4 = Mostly in place	**22–25** 5 = Fully in place

Notes and comments from the team:

8	**Data are routinely collected and systematically analyzed by the leadership team for program-evaluation and decision-making purposes.**
8.1	Staff collect and analyze patterns in ODRs using an electronic database.
8.2	Reports from the database are reviewed monthly to analyze patterns.
8.3	Staff collect and analyze information on students' social and academic behavior in classrooms and nonclassroom settings.
8.4	Data are analyzed to evaluate the relationship between ethnicity and disciplinary actions (e.g., referrals, suspensions, expulsions).
8.5	ODR data are analyzed in the screening process to identify students with or at risk of developing E/BPs.
8.6	ODR data are considered when developing intervention plans for students.

Place a tally mark to reflect each of the scores of individual team members, and circle the box that reflects the scores from most team members. If there is a significant discrepancy or a very low score, discuss the individual scores of the indicators to help to develop consensus.

6–9 1 = Not yet in place	**10–15** 2 = Partially in place	**16–20** 3 = Moderately in place	**21–26** 4 = Mostly in place	**27–30** 5 = Fully in place

Notes and comments from the team:

9	**Families are seen as partners in the development of their child's program.**
9.1	Family members are part of each child's team and are encouraged to participate in meetings and school activities.
9.2	Parents of children with significant behavioral concerns have access to a family support group when needed.
9.3	Families are supported in gaining access to additional community resources.
9.4	Family education programs and resources are available at the school.
9.5	A family's cultural and community perspective is valued and integrated into communication and student supports.

Place a tally mark to reflect each of the scores of individual team members, and circle the box that reflects the scores from most team members. If there is a significant discrepancy or a very low score, discuss the individual scores of the indicators to help to develop consensus.

5–8 1 = Not yet in place	**9–12** 2 = Partially in place	**13–17** 3 = Moderately in place	**18–21** 4 = Mostly in place	**22–25** 5 = Fully in place

Notes and comments from the team:

10	**Comprehensive plans are developed for students and families in need of intensive support.**
10.1	Students with severe behavior problems have timely access to medical, mental health, and other community social services.
10.2	A student's use of prescription medication is known by staff and is monitored frequently by school and family members.
10.3	Students with individualized education programs (IEPs) have goals and objectives for their social and emotional needs.
10.4	Professionals from other agencies serve on students' IEP teams as needed.
10.5	The school or district has a formal agreement with community agencies to provide services to meet the needs of students and their families.
10.6	Interagency teams develop, implement, and evaluate treatment plans that are family centered, based on strengths and needs, and sensitive to cultural and linguistic differences.
10.7	A family support liaison regularly contacts parents of students in need of intensive support.
10.8	A case manager coordinates all communication between the interagency team members.

Place a tally mark to reflect each of the scores of individual team members, and circle the box that reflects the scores from most team members. If there is a significant discrepancy or a very low score, discuss the individual scores of the indicators to help to develop consensus.

8–14 1 = Not yet in place	**15–21** 2 = Partially in place	**22–28** 3 = Moderately in place	**29–35** 4 = Mostly in place	**36–40** 5 = Fully in place

Notes and comments from the team:

SAPRpbis™

Action Plan

1. Review the results of the team evaluation and identify up to three evidence-based practices to focus on improving throughout the next year as part of your schoolwide PBIS system. Review the indicators of these practices to help you develop specific, measurable objectives for improvement. See *The SAPR-PBIS™ Manual* for examples and suggestions for developing an effective action plan as well as for strategies and resources to strengthen each of the practices.

2. In the space below, record these objectives, briefly summarize the activities related to addressing each objective, and outline a plan for measuring progress. Throughout the year, review progress made toward fully implementing these objectives. In order to visually display changes in the scores across time, the leadership team can enter the total scores for each evidence-based practice into a spreadsheet program after each meeting. This will allow the team to generate line or bar graphs that display changes in scores over time. This provides an "at-a-glance" summary of the team's ratings across time.

Objective 1	Activities	Evaluation
Objective 2	Activities	Evaluation
Objective 3	Activities	Evaluation